ALPINE SK

BY ASHLEY GISH

CREATIVE EDUCATION • CREATIVE PAPERBACKS

Published by Creative Education and Creative Paperbacks
P.O. Box 227, Mankato, Minnesota 56002
Creative Education and Creative Paperbacks are imprints of
The Creative Company
www.thecreativecompany.us

Design by The Design Lab
Production by Rachel Klimpel
Art direction by Rita Marshall
Printed in the United States of America

Photographs by Alamy (Jure Makovec, sportpoint), AP Images
(ASSOCIATED PRESS, Kyodo), Getty Images (Noah Clayton,
George Rinhart/Corbis Historical), iStockphoto (Bigandt_Photog-
raphy, Creativaimage, IlexImage, technotr), Shutterstock (AS-kom,
Mikael Damkier, GTS Productions, JOZEF_KAROLY)

Library of Congress Cataloging-in-Publication Data
Names: Gish, Ashley, author.
Title: Alpine skiing / Ashley Gish.
Series: Amazing Winter Olympics.
Includes bibliographical references and index.
Summary: Celebrate the Winter Games with this high-interest intro-
duction to alpine skiing, the sport known for its slalom and downhill
races. Also included is a biographical story about skier Mikaela
Shiffrin.

Identifiers:
ISBN 978-1-64026-492-2 (hardcover)
ISBN 978-1-68277-044-3 (pbk)
ISBN 978-1-64000-622-5 (eBook)
This title has been submitted for CIP processing under LCCN
2021937335.

First Edition HC 9 8 7 6 5 4 3 2 1
First Edition PBK 9 8 7 6 5 4 3 2 1

Table of Contents

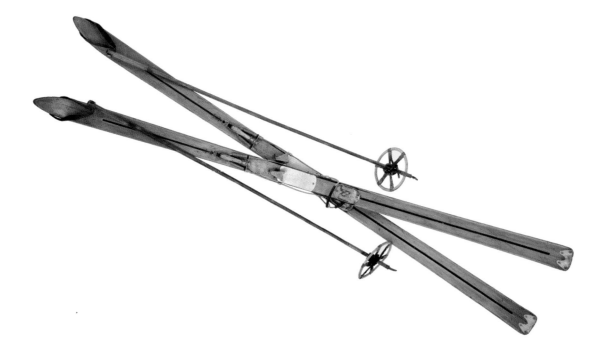

Alpine skiing became part of the Winter Olympic Games in 1936. That year, the games included one men's event and one women's event. Since then, more events have been added.

In 1936, the Winter Olympics took place in Bavaria, Germany.

Racers crouch and lean forward to gain speed while staying focused on the course ahead.

Racers try to be **aerodynamic**. This helps them ski faster. They crouch low. They tuck their ski poles against their bodies. They wear formfitting speedsuits, too.

aerodynamic having a shape that allows air to move past without pushing the body back

Bindings are set to "release" a ski in certain conditions if a skier falls.

Competitors wear fixed-heel skis. Bindings secure the skier's boots to the skis. These athletes also wear helmets, goggles, gloves, and shin guards.

Groomed snow is often called corduroy because it looks like the ridges of corduroy fabric.

Many alpine skiers train and compete on a **piste** (*PEEST*). Snow-grooming vehicles smooth and pack down the snow on pistes. This improves conditions for racers.

piste a track for winter sports made from packed snow

A "run" is one pass down the ski slope. Some events are decided after just one run. Others involve two or more runs. Championship course lengths are one to three miles (1.6–4.8 km), start to finish.

The men's downhill course is usually 1.5 to 3 miles (2.4–4.8 km) long.

Racers try to turn as narrowly as possible to keep up their speed.

The Olympics feature five types of alpine ski races. **Slalom** and giant slalom races have many curves and turns. The super giant slalom (super-G) and downhill are longer, faster races. The combined event involves both downhill and slalom.

slalom a downhill race over a winding or zigzag course marked by gates

Cross-blocking is a tactic skiers use to knock gates out of their way as they pass.

During slaloms, competitors steer between **gates**. The gates are set farther apart in giant slaloms. Gates are set farthest apart for the super-G. Racers often ski so close to the gates that they hit them with their hands or shins.

gates flexible poles used in winter sports

ALPINE SKIING

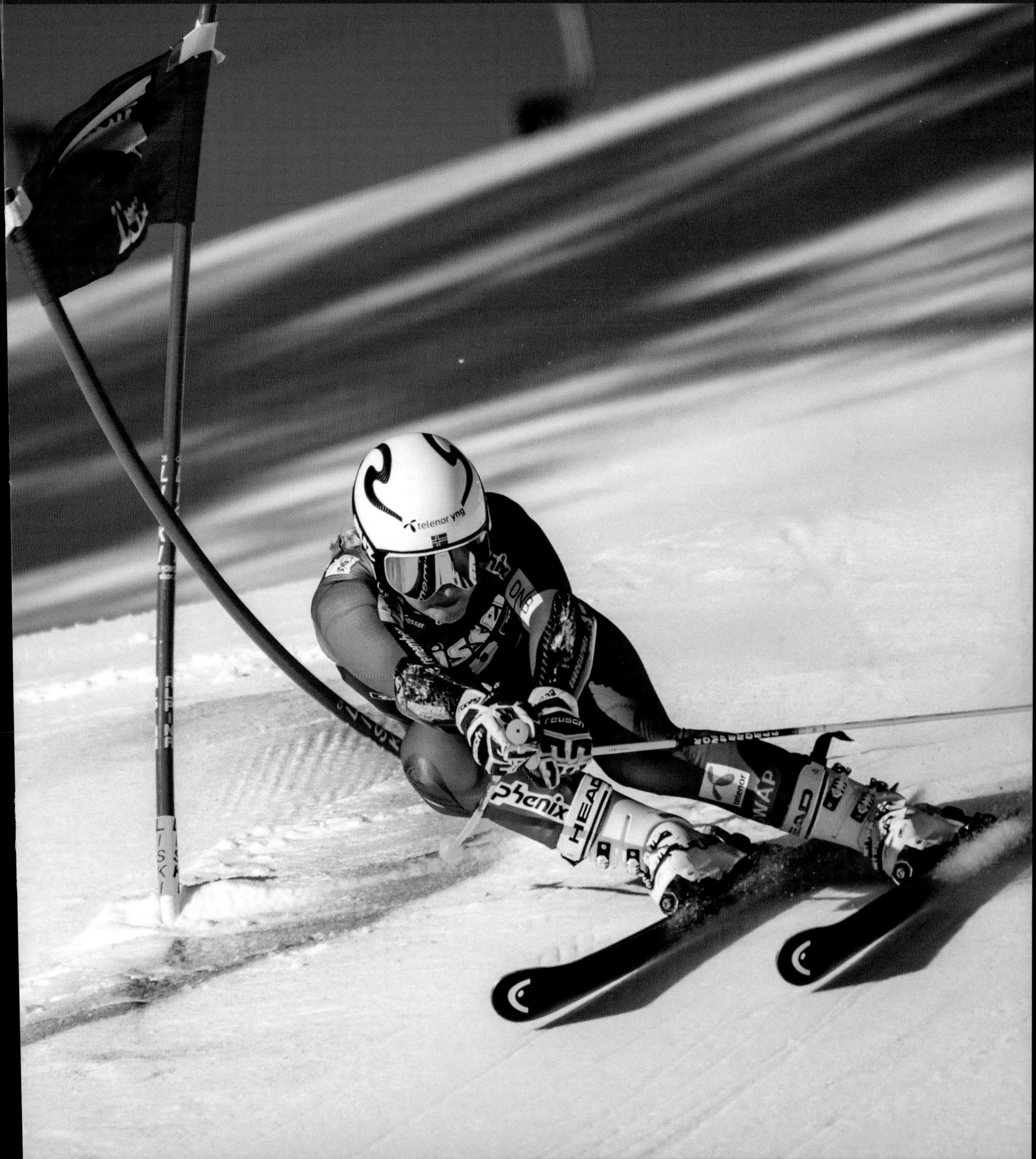
telenor yng
phenix
HEAD
telenor

Downhill racing is all about speed. Racers may reach speeds of up to 95 miles (153 km) per hour on these steep courses. Some curvy downhill courses have jumps that send skiers flying through the air!

Some courses are marked by as many as 75 gates!

As of 2021, Austria, Switzerland, and the United States had won the most gold medals in the Olympics for alpine skiing. Millions of fans around the world watch athletes compete in this exciting sport!

Norway won the most medals in the 2018 Winter Olympics, held in Pyeongchang, South Korea.

Competitor Spotlight: Mikaela Shiffrin

Mikaela

Shiffrin began alpine skiing as a professional at age 15. In 2011, she claimed third place in the World Cup. She was just 16. Since then, she has won many competitions. In 2018, she became the youngest ski racer to win 50 World Cup races. As of 2021, Shiffrin had won two gold medals and one silver medal in the Winter Olympics.

Read More

Fishman, Jon M. *Mikaela Shiffrin*. Minneapolis: Lerner, 2015.

Labrecque, Ellen. *Alpine Skiing*. Ann Arbor, Mich.: Cherry Lake, 2018.

Waxman, Laura Hamilton. *Skiing*. North Mankato, Minn.: Amicus, 2018.

Websites

Kiddle: Skiing Facts for Kids
https://kids.kiddle.co/Skiing
Find out more about the history of skiing.

US Ski & Snowboard: Mikaela Shiffrin
https://usskiandsnowboard.org/athletes/mikaela-shiffrin
Read about the Olympic gold medalist, and watch videos of some of her runs.

Note: Every effort has been made to ensure that the websites listed above are suitable for children, that they have educational value, and that they contain no inappropriate material. However, because of the nature of the Internet, it is impossible to guarantee that these sites will remain active indefinitely or that their contents will not be altered.

Index